Mary Slessor

What is it like?

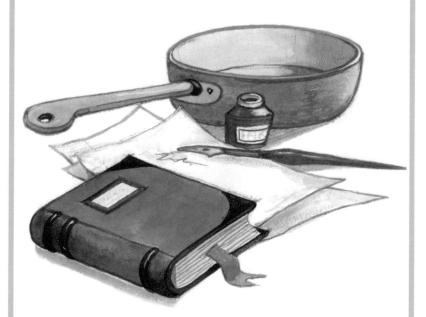

The true story of Mary Slessor
and her African adventure

Catherine Mackenzie
Illustrated by Rita Ammassari

Mary Slessor was a Scottish lass with fiery red hair and a spirit of adventure. Her family had moved to the city of Dundee to get a better life. However, when they arrived, Mary's dad still didn't get a job; he still hit her mother and there still wasn't enough food to go round. Nothing had changed that much. Mary had to leave school to work in the jute mill. They made rope there.

'What's the mill like?' Mary's little sister asked when she got home. Mary wiped her brow and sighed, 'Dirty, noisy and exhausting.'

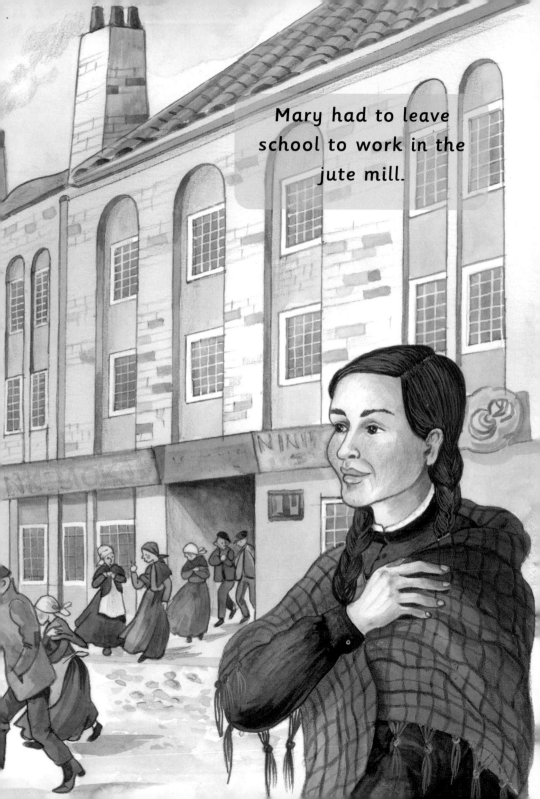

Mary had to leave school to work in the jute mill.

Mary's mother had some exciting news one day. 'They're starting evening classes at the mill.' Mary couldn't wait to go. She learned lots of things there. On the globe she would look at the different countries you could travel to.

'What's it like in Africa?' Mary asked her mother as they came home from church on Sunday.

'Many people in Africa don't know that God sent his only Son to this world to save them from sin,' Mary's mother replied.

Mary frowned. 'Shouldn't someone tell them?' she wondered.

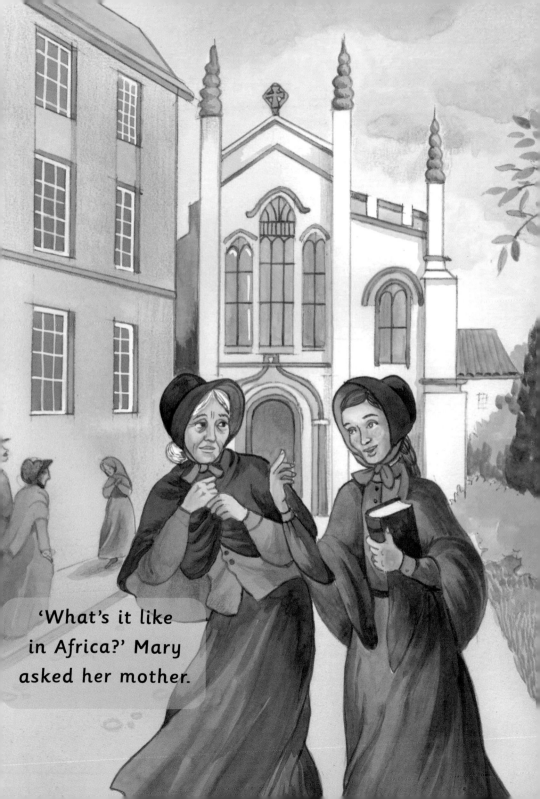

'What's it like in Africa?' Mary asked her mother.

As she grew up, Mary spent a lot of time helping out at church. She loved Jesus and longed for others to love him too. One day, when Mary was walking to church, some lads started to pester her. One boy had a big lead weight on a string and was handling it as if it were a weapon.

Mary stood her ground. Raising her voice she exclaimed, 'Swing that lead weight as close to my face as possible. If I flinch you win – but if I stick it out then you have to come to church with me.'

The boys thought they would win for sure. But they didn't. Mary walked into church with the lads following her.

One boy had a big lead weight on a string.

The people of Calabar, however, were never far from Mary's mind. Mary wanted to be a missionary. And that is what happened.

'I don't know what it's really going to be like in Africa,' Mary said to her mother, as she waved goodbye at the door. 'But I do know that this is what God wants me to do and that he will be with me always.'

'I don't know what it's really going to be like in Africa', Mary said to her mother.

It was hard going at first. There was a long ocean journey and Duke Town, where she stayed at first, was hot and humid. She had to learn a different language and Mary was shocked at the way women and children were treated.

A lot of the tribes worshipped false gods. Some believed that if a woman gave birth to twins, one of them was a child of the devil. They would then take one of the babies, or both of them, and leave them to be killed by wild animals.

Mary was shocked at
the way women and
children were treated.

When Mary had learned the language, she left to start a new mission station in the jungle. She went to stay in Old Town, in a little mud hut. Some of the people there were friendly, but some were not. However, those who really listened to what Mary had to say respected her. They gave Mary the nickname of 'Ma' because of their deep love for her.

When they heard news of abandoned babies they would warn Mary. She would then sneak into the jungle to rescue them. Some of these boys and girls were adopted by Mary as her very own family.

She went to stay in Old Town, in a little mud hut.

One day, Mary was travelling in a canoe on the river. Some men were there to help row and steer the boat. When they were in the middle of the river, a terrible sight met their eyes. A huge hippopotamus emerged from underneath their boat. Its mouth was wide open and its teeth were as big as gravestones.

Mary took things into her own hands. Finding a saucepan in her travel sack, she whacked the hippopotamus over the head and yelled, 'Get away ya brute!' The hippopotamus got such a shock, it promptly disappeared under the water again.

A huge hippopotamus emerged from underneath their boat.

Mary's days were busy with teaching, medical care and giving wise advice whether it was asked for or not. She would even give advice to the local chief, King Eyo. But he didn't mind. He was a Christian and a great help to Mary in her work. The nights were busy too. If there wasn't sick people to heal, or babies to rescue, there was always the need to pray.

At night, on the dirt floor of some mud hut in the middle of the jungle, she would simply call out to God. 'Oh Lord, there are so many villages that need to hear about you and your Son, Jesus. Help me reach them!'

'Oh Lord, there are
so many villages
that need to hear
about you and your
Son, Jesus.'

One of the tribes she wanted to reach was the Okoyong. However, when King Eyo heard that she planned to live with this fierce tribe, he was worried. 'They will kill you,' he exclaimed.

But Mary was tough. 'What must it be like for these people who know nothing of Jesus Christ and God's love?'

King Eyo relented, but only if Mary agreed to travel there in his special canoe.

Mary accepted Eyo's offer. Then when she arrived, she realised how terrible this tribe really was. They were violent and cruel to themselves and others. 'These poor people don't even know what love is,' Mary gasped. 'I must tell them about the love of Christ.'

'These poor people don't even know what love is,' Mary gasped.

The Okoyong didn't want to listen at first. Mary told them again and again about God's love, but all they wanted was violence. One day, as she rushed in on a battle about to start, the warriors yelled at her, 'Out of the way, Ma! We fight. You die too. Move on!'

Mary simply yelled back, 'Shoot if you dare!'

She wouldn't budge. The warriors didn't know what to do. Mary ordered the warring sides to sit down and talk about their differences. While they did this, Mary knitted. After hours of talking, the warriors went home exhausted. Mary went home with a blanket for one of the children.

Mary ordered the warring sides to sit down and talk about their differences.

In time, many in the Okoyong tribe stopped their fighting and accepted God's love. That was when Mary decided to go and live with the Azo. 'They will kill you,' the Okoyong exclaimed. 'Do you know what it will be like there?' Mary nodded. She knew that the Azo were just like the Okoyong, who were just like the people from Scotland, who were just like sinners from any country in the world. All people are sinners and all people need Christ.

The Azo were the last tribe that Mary ever travelled to. Many of them came to trust in Jesus. Some time later, Mary died amongst the people she loved and the country she called home. Africa had been her home for many years – but now heaven was.

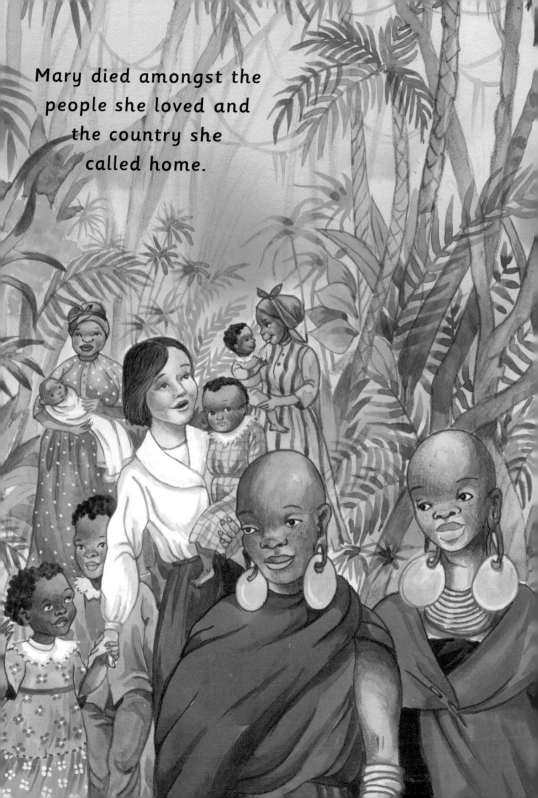

Mary died amongst the
people she loved and
the country she
called home.

This book is written for Lydia, Esther, Philip, Lois, Jack, Marianne, Isobel and Elizabeth.

May grace and peace be multiplied to you in the knowledge of God and of Jesus our Lord (2 Peter 1:2 ESV).

10 9 8 7 6 5 4 3
Copyright © 2012 Catherine Mackenzie
ISBN: 978-1-84550-791-6
Reprinted in 2016 and 2020

Published by Christian Focus Publications,
Geanies House, Fearn, Tain, Ross-shire, IV20 1TW,
Scotland, U.K.
www.christianfocus.com

Cover design by Daniel van Straaten
Illustrated by Rita Ammassari
Printed in China